LANDMARKS OF DEMOCRACY
AMERICAN INSTITUTIONS

THE INTERNAL REVENUE SERVICE

WHY U.S. CITIZENS PAY TAXES

JASON BAROUSSE

PowerKiDS
press

New York

Published in 2018 by The Rosen Publishing Group, Inc.
29 East 21st Street, New York, NY 10010

First Edition

Editor: Elizabeth Krajnik
Book Design: Reann Nye

Photo Credits: Cover, pp. 14, 21 Rob Crandall/Shutterstock.com; p. 4 bakdc/ Shutterstock.com; p. 5 Courtesy of the Library of Congress; p. 6 https://commons. wikimedia.org/wiki/File:Grover_Cleveland_-_NARA_-_518139_(cropped).jpg; p. 7 https://commons.wikimedia.org/wiki/File:Grover_Cleveland_and_Wilson-Gorman_Tariff_Cartoon.jpg; p. 8 https://commons.wikimedia.org/wiki/File:William_Howard_Taft_1909b.jpg; p. 9 https://commons.wikimedia.org/wiki/File:-Puck_cartoon_of_Senator_Nelson_Aldrich.jpg_1906.jpg; p. 11 https://commons. wikimedia.org/wiki/File:16th_Amendment_Pg1of1_AC.jpg; p. 12 https://commons. wikimedia.org/wiki/File:Pump1913.jpg; p. 13 Keystone-France/Gamma-Keystone/ Getty Images; p. 15 https://commons.wikimedia.org/wiki/File:Federal_Triangle_ USGS_2002.jpg; p. 16 Spectruminfo/Shutterstock.com; p. 17 WAYHOME studio/ Shutterstock.com; p. 18 Andrey_Popov/Shutterstock.com; p. 19 Ollyy/Shutterstock. com; p. 22 PTstock/Shutterstock.com.

Cataloging-in-Publication Data

Names: Barousse, Jason.
Title: The Internal Revenue Service: why U.S. citizens pay taxes / Jason Barousse.
Description: New York : PowerKids Press, 2018. | Series: Landmarks of democracy: American institutions | Includes index.
Identifiers: ISBN 9781508161394 (pbk.) | ISBN 9781508161417 (library bound) | ISBN 9781508161400 (6 pack)
Subjects: LCSH: United States. Internal Revenue Service–History–Juvenile literature. | United States. Internal Revenue Service. | Income tax–United States–History–Juvenile literature. | Taxation–United States – Juvenile literature.
Classification: LCC HJ2361.B37 2018 | DDC 336.240973–dc23

Manufactured in the United States of America

CPSIA Compliance Information: Batch #BS17PK: For Further Information contact Rosen Publishing, New York, New York at 1-800-237-9932

CONTENTS

PAYING FOR THE WAR

The American Civil War, which lasted from 1861 to 1865, cost the United States about $4.2 billion (more than $60 billion in today's dollars). The **Revenue** Act of 1861 authorized the government to put a federal income tax into place. This tax was meant to help pay for the Civil War.

The Revenue Act of 1862 replaced the Revenue Act of 1861. The new act created the position of the commissioner of **internal** revenue. George S. Boutwell, a former Massachusetts governor, was the first person appointed to this position. He served for just eight months. The commissioner works in the Department of the U.S. **Treasury**.

DEPARTMENT OF THE U.S. TREASURY BUILDING
WASHINGTON, D.C.

Boutwell's job as the first commissioner of internal revenue was to organize the Bureau of Internal Revenue, which is now known as the Internal Revenue Service, or IRS.

INDECISION ABOUT INCOME TAX

The first hints at the government's indecision about having an income tax came with the debate surrounding the Revenue Act of 1861 and the Revenue Act of 1862. The income tax wasn't meant to last forever, but it was renewed in 1866, 1867, and 1870.

GROVER CLEVELAND

INSTITUTION INSIGHT

The Revenue Act of 1894, or the Wilson-Gorman **Tariff** Act of 1894, was meant to **reform** U.S. tariffs. It included an income tax meant to replace the money lost from reducing tariffs. This bill became law without President Grover Cleveland's signature. In 1895, the Supreme Court ruled that the income tax section of the act was unconstitutional and it was removed.

This political cartoon was featured on the cover of *Harper's Weekly* on September 8, 1894. It shows President Grover Cleveland pushing a chariot with Senator Arthur Pue Gorman in it. The chariot is crushing Congressman William Wilson and his low-tariff bill.

Ten years after it passed the Revenue Act of 1861, Congress **repealed** the income tax. The economy was getting stronger again in the years after the Civil War and it was difficult for government leaders to prove an income tax was necessary. At the end of 1871, the income tax ended.

AMENDING THE CONSTITUTION

Repealing the Civil War-era income tax did not get rid of an income tax forever. Although this first tax was intended to pay for the war, the government later saw benefits to **reinstating** an income tax. However, the Constitution prevented taxes that weren't **imposed** upon the states based on their population.

President William Taft and a number of other government officials realized that the Constitution would have to be amended to make an income tax legal. However, this income tax wouldn't be based on population. The 16th Amendment was introduced in 1909 to begin the process of creating a constitutional income tax.

WILLIAM TAFT

This political cartoon from *Puck* magazine in 1906 shows Senator Nelson Aldrich as a spider that traps and destroys important laws. Nelson supported corporate taxes as a way to defeat the income tax.

RATIFYING THE 16TH AMENDMENT

Both houses of Congress approved Taft's suggested amendment to the Constitution. In July 1909, the 16th Amendment was passed along to each state to be ratified, or approved. Three-fourths of the states in the Union needed to ratify it.

Alabama was the first state to ratify the 16th Amendment. It took nearly four years for enough states to ratify it. In February 1913, Delaware became the 36th state to ratify the amendment, putting it into effect.

⊙ INSTITUTION INSIGHT

At the time the 16th Amendment was sent to each state's government in 1909, there were only 46 states in the Union, making the three-fourths majority 35 states. In 1912, the Union added Arizona and New Mexico. This increased the three-fourths majority to 36 states.

Sixty-first Congress of the United States of America;

At the First Session,

Begun and held at the City of Washington on Monday, the fifteenth day of March,
one thousand nine hundred and nine.

JOINT RESOLUTION

Proposing an amendment to the Constitution of the United States.

I certify that this Joint Resolution originated in the Senate.

*Resolved by the Senate and House of Representatives of the United States
of America in Congress assembled (two-thirds of each House concurring
therein),* That the following article is proposed as an amendment to the
Constitution of the United States, which, when ratified by the legislatures of
three-fourths of the several States, shall be valid to all intents and purposes as a
part of the Constitution:

"ARTICLE XVI. The Congress shall have power to lay and collect taxes
on incomes, from whatever source derived, without apportionment among the
several States, and without regard to any census or enumeration."

Speaker of the House of Representatives.

*Vice-President of the United States and
President of the Senate.*

Attest:

Clerk of the House of Representatives.

Charles G. Bennett

By Henry H. Gilfry
Secretary

The 16th Amendment started the process that
led to a new federal income tax.

11

RAISING THE INCOME TAX

President Woodrow Wilson signed the Revenue Act of 1913 on October 3, 1913. This act allowed the collection of a federal income tax. However, some changes have been made to it since it was put into place.

This political cartoon from 1914 shows President Woodrow Wilson pouring laws into a pump to make businesses more prosperous.

President Franklin D. Roosevelt, pictured here, claimed that the Revenue Act of 1942, which increased the tax rate and the amount of Americans who needed to pay taxes, was "the greatest tax bill in American history."

During World War I, the Revenue Act of 1918 raised the top level of the income tax to 77 percent. After the war ended, the top rate fell to just 24 percent in 1929. But America was shaken by the stock market crash of October 1929, which caused lawmakers to raise taxes once again. Taxes rose even higher during World War II.

13

FROM THE BUREAU OF INTERNAL REVENUE TO THE IRS

For many years, the U.S. government was powered by the spoils system. This system was a way for political parties to reward their supporters and campaign workers. After a party won an election, party leaders would hire these supporters to fill government jobs.

In 1953, President Dwight Eisenhower changed the agency's name from the Bureau of Internal Revenue to the Internal Revenue Service.

The IRS building in Washington, D.C., was designed by architect Louis A. Simon and constructed from 1928 to 1936. This building was the first to be built within the Federal Triangle area. Many of the buildings in the Federal Triangle were constructed as part of a building project that greatly changed downtown Washington, D.C., throughout the mid-20th century.

IRS BUILDING

The Bureau of Internal Revenue operated on the spoils system until the 1950s, when the agency began hiring professionals. About this time,

OTHER TAXES

Americans pay a number of different types of taxes. When people think of taxes, they most often think about income tax. Working citizens pay income tax directly from their paychecks. In addition to federal income taxes, most states also require residents to pay state income tax.

Other taxes include property tax and sales tax. People and businesses pay property taxes to the county, city, or town in which they live or are located. Sales tax is a percentage applied to the things we buy or activities we pay for. It is determined by each state. Sometimes local governments also add a sales tax.

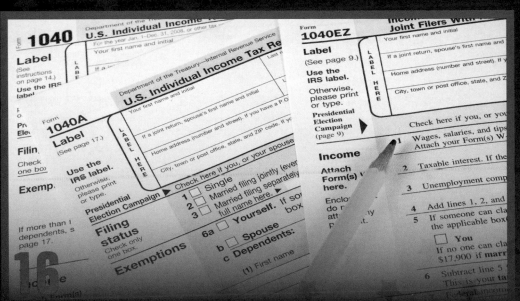

When people file their federal and state income tax returns, they sometimes get money back from one or both governments. This is called a tax refund.

KNOW YOUR RIGHTS

Understanding taxes can be difficult. Knowing your rights as a taxpayer is very important. The IRS has created a taxpayer bill of rights so that American citizens can be informed when dealing with the IRS.

INSTITUTION INSIGHT

Some people file their own tax returns. Other people choose to hire a professional **accountant** to do their taxes for them. These people are well informed about changes in tax rules.

The IRS performs audits on some people. An audit is when the IRS has found an issue with a person's tax return and wants to review their records.

The taxpayer bill of rights lists a set of 10 rights that every taxpayer should be aware of. People have the right to be informed, to receive quality service, to pay no more than the correct amount of tax, to challenge the IRS's position and be heard, to appeal an IRS decision in an independent **forum**, to have finality or completion, to have privacy, to have **confidentiality**, to retain representation, and to expect a fair and just tax system.

WHAT DO TAXES PAY FOR TODAY?

The money Americans pay in taxes is part of the government's revenue. The government spends this money on a number of different things. In 2015, the United States took in $3.18 trillion, nearly half of which came from individual income taxes.

The government breaks that money down into three spending categories: **interest** on federal **debt**, **discretionary** spending (the amount of money the government can spend from the budget approved by Congress), and **mandatory** spending (money that doesn't come from the budget approved by Congress). In 2015, the largest area of discretionary spending was the military and the largest area of mandatory spending was Social Security, unemployment, and labor.

INSTITUTION INSIGHT

Cutting government spending is one way to reduce the government's debt. However, many of the programs the government spends money on are very important. If the government cuts these programs, many federal employees could lose their jobs and many people could lose the benefits of programs such as Social Security or veterans' benefits.

Just like cutting government spending, cutting the amount people pay in taxes can have unfavorable effects. Without tax money, the U.S. government has a smaller income and a smaller budget, and therefore less money to spend on government programs.

UNITED STATES

Internal Revenue Service Building

21

TAXES IN THE FUTURE

Each new president makes a new set of promises to the American population. It is the president's job to make sure that the U.S. government can afford to take care of its citizens. Many presidents in the past have promised to cut government spending and taxes.

Cutting taxes can cause many unfavorable side effects. For example, it could prevent people from collecting their Social Security benefits in the future. Cutting funding for government programs can be dangerous, too. Without government-funded programs, the United States will not be able to serve its citizens.

GLOSSARY

accountant: Someone whose job is keeping the financial records of a person or a business.

confidentiality: The quality of being kept secret or private.

debt: Money owed to another.

discretionary: Available to be used when and how someone decides.

forum: A place or opportunity for discussion.

impose: To force someone to accept or put up with something.

interest: The profit made on money that is loaned to someone.

internal: Of or relating to the home affairs of a country or organization.

mandatory: Required.

reform: To improve something by removing faults or problems.

reinstate: To put something back in place.

repeal: To do away with a law.

revenue: Money that is made by or paid to a business or organization.

tariff: Taxes placed by a government on goods coming into a country.

treasury: A government department in charge of finances.

INDEX

WEBSITES

Due to the changing nature of Internet links, PowerKids Press has developed an online list of websites related to the subject of this book. This site is updated regularly. Please use this link to access the list: www.powerkidslinks.com/lod/irs